Table of Contents

HISTORIC HOMES
CHARLESTON • SOUTH CAROLINA

South Battery

CHARLESTON was founded in 1670 and is the oldest city between Virginia and Florida. It was the first capital of the Carolinas and of South Carolina. The young settlement on the west bank of the Ashley River was named Charles Town for King Charles I of England. Charles II granted a charter for a vast area of this new country and called it Carolina, a derivative of Carolus, Latin for Charles, to honor himself. In 1672, plantation owners Henry Hughes and John Coming donated half their land on Oyster Point between the Ashley and Cooper Rivers and the city was relocated across the Ashley River to the Charleston peninsula. The "Grand Modell," a plan of the "New Charles Town" designed by Lord Ashley Cooper, specified lot sizes and street widths. It was drawn to "avoid the undecent and incommodious irregularities which other English colonies are fallen into for want of an early care in laying out the Townes."

Originally called Fort Street, South Battery was a narrow bit of a street running between Church Street and Meeting Street. Today, its historic houses face the site of Ft. Sumter in the distant harbor, where the War Between the States began.

South Battery

Much of Charleston's early prosperity was built on Indian trade, rice, indigo and shipping. Softly tanned deerskins were in high demand for breeches and hats. Experimentally planted rice and indigo became major cash and export crops in the 1730's and 40's. Many of Charleston's merchants soon amassed some of the largest private fortunes of America's Colonial period. Many homes constructed in this period served as places of business as well as dwellings, the second and third floors reserved for family, the main floor for business. The prosperity of their owners was reflected in grand architectural designs.

The exterior of *32 South Battery* features a prominent cupola and a two tiered piazza. The interior is graced with Regency period detailing. The home is believed to have been built for Col. John Ashe in 1782 by a Mr. Miller, credited with design and construction of a number of Charleston's fine homes during that era.

30 South Battery was built in 1860 by James E. Spear. The three story residence is a fine example of Italianate architecture, adapted to the sub-tropical climate of the Carolinas through the addition of piazzas, or shaded porches.

Most of Charleston's elegantly massive homes sit shoulder to shoulder on tiny lots, a carry-over from the crowded European lifestyle the settlers left behind.

32 South Battery

30 South Battery

South Battery

*T*HE beautiful homes along South Battery are an elegant mixture of architectural designs. *20 South Battery* was built in 1843 by Samuel N. Stevens, a prosperous factor. It was remodeled and enlarged in 1870 in Second Empire style for Col. Richard Lathers, a millionaire cotton broker, banker, insurance executive and railroad director, who later served in the Union Army. After the war, Lathers wined and dined military and political leaders at the mansion in an effort to reconcile the nation. His attempts failed. In 1874 he sold the residence to Andrew Simonds, a local banker, and moved North.

22 South Battery, Italianate in design, was built in 1858 for Nathaniel Russell Middleton, a planter.

The home at *24 South Battery* is the western half of an 18th Century double tenement. The eastern half was torn down to accommodate Middleton's home. The building was remodeled in 1870.

The Georgian style home at *8 South Battery* was built in 1768 by Thomas Savage. It was later purchased by Col. William Washington, kinsman of George Washington.

The Italian Villa style mansion at *26 South Battery* was built in 1853 for Col. John Algernon Sydney Ashe. The home features arcades and bracketed cornices.

The home at *28 South Battery* is a stuccoed brick villa built by George S. Cook, the noted photographer, in 1860.

20 South Battery

24 · 22 South Battery

26 South Battery

20 South Battery

8 South Battery

28 South Battery

South Battery

Four South Battery, an Italian Renaissance Revival style design of F.P. Dinkelberg of New York, was built in 1892-93 by Maj. Andrew Simonds, president of the First National Bank and commodore of the Carolina Yacht Club, for his young bride. In 1909 it became, for a time, the hotel Villa Margherita.

The Stucco house at *2 South Battery* dates from 1905 and was built for the O'Neill sisters. The rear portion encompasses the carriage house of 1 East Battery.

The Magwood-Moreland House at *39 South Battery* was built in 1827. Whether by design or chance, it was built on a foundation of criss-crossed palmetto poles. Some claim the builder intentionally designed the home to be hurricane proof. Others believe the home was constructed atop the remains of a palmetto log fort. Whichever story is accurate, the palmetto foundation allows the house to sway slightly, making it virtually earthquake proof. It was among the homes that survived the 1886 earthquake that leveled most of Charleston. Residents of the Magwood-Moreland home today claim they can still feel a slight sway during gale or hurricane force winds, a testament to the quality and creativity that went into the marvelous homes of this era.

4 South Battery

2 South Battery

39 South Battery

South Battery

*F*OURTY-NINE *South Battery* is believed to have been constructed in 1795 by Col. James English and was occupied by several generations of his descendants. The home is a classic example of the single house style, a unique Charleston design consisting of a house one room wide and two deep, with the narrow end facing the street. A one or two story piazza, designed to catch the cooling sea breezes, was usually added to the side of this type of home. Like many Charleston homes, the entry does not open directly into the house but onto the piazza.

The piazza, as defined by Samuel Johnson in 1750, is "a walk under a roof supported by pillars." Like much of the city's plans and architecture, it is borrowed directly from England. The first piazza was built by architect Inigo Jones at Covent Garden in London. Not only offering a bit of much needed shade to Charleston's homes, the piazza also provided an intimate view of the city's street life. Both airy and functional, the piazza gave builders the opportunity to add graceful columns, capitals and fancy woodwork to the face of otherwise rather austere structures. Unusually, both *44 and 46 South Battery* turn their delightful double piazzas to the street.

49 South Battery

49 South Battery

46 South Battery

44 South Battery

South Battery

$\mathcal{M}$OST of Charleston's homes were constructed either very near or right up against the sidewalk line, allowing for little or no room for plantings. The side or rear yards of the homes, artistically fenced, became sheltered and wonderfully lush flower and herb gardens. These gardens were tended by the ladies of the house, usually with the assistance of household slaves.

The house at *56 South Battery* is believed to be of post-revolutionary construction. It has since been remodeled featuring an elegant ironwork second floor piazza. Intricately styled hand wrought iron was used to provide gates, fences and balustrades for many of Charleston's Colonial period homes. Much of this craftsmanship was lost in the 1886 earthquake but enough survived to inspire artisans in the Nineteenth century when cast iron was added to hand wrought work.

During 1984 and 1985, the house and garden at *58 South Battery*, built in 1800 for John Black, was completely restored. Using original diagrams, wrought iron gates, and bricks excavated from the yard, the garden was reconstructed to its splendid beauty.

William Gibbes built *64 South Battery* sometime between 1772 and 1788. A merchant, shipowner and planter, he built a large wharf in front of the house. The gardens were designed by Mrs. Washington A. Roebling, whose husband along with his father, John August Roebling, designed and built the Brooklyn Bridge in 1869-83.

74 South Battery

95 South Battery

56 South Battery

64 South Battery

58 South Battery

Murray Blvd.

Murray Boulevard was named for Andrew Buist Murray, an orphan who became a successful businessman and philanthropist as well as a Charleston benefactor. The 47 acres behind this waterfront boulevard are reclaimed mud flats developed into building lots in 1911. Murray also proposed lengthening East Battery to connect with the boulevard by extending the seawall south of White Point Gardens. This created a lovely riverside boulevard over a mile in length. Murray, at no profit to himself, contributed nearly 50% of the cost of the development.

In the Eighteenth and early Nineteenth centuries, builders lavished a great deal of care, craftsmanship and attention to detail on the staircases, porticos and doorways of Charleston's homes. The double-curving stairs of *28 Murray* and semicircular pillared entrances of it and *46 Murray* reflect the refined tastes of their first owners. Another sign of wealth and good taste was the addition of massive columns to support and accent the piazzas and entrances as seen in several Murray Boulevard homes. Columns were often topped with ornate establature in Roman or Greek styles.

28 Murray Boulevard

46 Murray Boulevard

36 Murray Boulevard

32 Murray Boulevard

Murray Blvd.

$\mathcal{T}$HE home at *52 Murray* was the first to be built on the new boulevard. The imposing Colonial Revival residence was built by C. Bissel Jenkins, one of the pioneers of the Reclamation Movement. The 15 room home, built of Summerville brick with red Ludovici tile roofing, was designed by Walker & Burden Architects. It did not stand alone long and was soon joined by other imposing structures featuring the architectural styles popular in the early 1900's. By the mid-1900's Murray Boulevard bore no resemblance to the area at nearby White Point where famous pirate of the high seas Stede Bonnet was hanged.

In 1718, Edward Teach, alias Blackbeard, arrived off the coast of Charleston with a fleet of pirate ships. His buccaneers seized several merchant ships, capturing, among others Councilman Samuel Wragg and his son. The prisoners were held for ransom. Teach was captured and executed by Virginia authorities. The residents of Charleston did achieve some measure of revenge, however, when Col. William Rhett captured the cut-throat Bonnet and his men in the Cape Fear River. They were tried before Justice Nicholas Trott and hanged on White Point. The bodies were buried below the high water mark on the point.

74 Murray Boulevard

62 Murray Boulevard

46 Murray Boulevard

52 Murray Boulevard

Church St.

CHURCH Street, named for St. Philip's Church, was part of the original "Grand Modell" for Charles Town in 1672. The houses that continue to stand on Church Street exemplify over three centuries of Charleston's history. *41 Church*, as legend would have it, was built in 1909 on a wager. Architect A.W. Todd was bet that he could not build a respectably large dwelling on a narrow 25 by 150 foot lot - a bet he handily won. An interesting feature of the lovely home is the garage entrance built through the chimney.

39 Church was built nearly two centuries earlier, in 1743 for George Eveleigh. The two and one-half story stuccoed house is built of small bricks and follows an asymmetrical floor plan, popular in early houses. A tornado in 1811 tore away a 30 foot roof beam and drove it into the roof of a house on King Street a quarter of a mile away. The house also once had a secret staircase leading from a cupboard in the drawing room to the closet in a room below, perhaps a lifesaving feature in revolutionary times.

32 Church was built by Robert Lindsay, a carpenter, in the early 1800's.

41 Church St.

39 Church St.

30 Church St.

32 Church St.

31 Church St.

Church St.

THE entrance to *55 Church* is another example of the fine workmanship and eye for detail that went into creating inviting entrances to the lovely homes on Charleston's streets.

71 Church, of three story stuccoed brick construction, is one of the earliest surviving examples of Charleston single houses. It was built by Col. Robert Brewton perhaps as early as 1721. Brewton was the son of Col. Miles Brewton who fought in the war against the Yemassee Indians in 1715. Col. Robert Brewton was a wealthy wharf owner, a militia officer and a member of the Commons House of Assembly.

59 Church was built by Thomas Rose, an Ashley River planter in 1733, soon after his marriage. It is said the house is haunted by the ghost of Dr. Joseph Brown Ladd who died in a duel defending the honor of a traveling actress nicknamed "Perdita." Mortally wounded by his one time friend Ralph Isaacs, Dr. Ladd died in the house three weeks later, long after the lady in question had left town.

69 Church is a classic example of the double house, almost literally two single houses built together creating a nearly square structure with a room in each corner and a central hall or side hall with a grand staircase, often visible from the front door. The house's ancestry is clouded but it may have been built in 1745 by Richard Capers, a planter, for his third wife. The only public record of the house indicates that Jacob Motte, the Public Treasurer, leased the house from 1761 until his death in 1770.

55 Church Street

71 Church Street

59 Church Street

69 Church Street

Church St.

THE Georgian brick house at *87 Church* was built in 1772 by Daniel Heyward, a rice planter, for his son Thomas, a British-educated attorney, patriot and signer of the Declaration of Independence. In 1791 President George Washington stayed here while visiting the city. In 1794, John Grimke purchased the house. Two of Grimke's daughters later played an active role in the abolitionist movement. Owned by The Charleston Museum, the house is open to the public.

The house at *78 Church* was combined with *76* to create one dwelling. It was in *76 Church* that DuBose Heyward wrote "Porgy," the novel which became the wildly popular operetta "Porgy and Bess." It is believed that President George Washington spoke to the people of Charleston from the balcony of *78 Church* when he visited the city in 1791. The present balcony, however, is in the Regency style of 1815-25. An antique mahogany bedpost partially supports the third floor of this home, proof of the ingenuity of Charleston's residents in overcoming the adversity and hard times that besieged the city after the Revolution.

87 Church Street

74 Church Street

78 Church Street

Church St.

NINETY-TWO Church is a three and one half story brick Adamesque home built in 1805 by Alexander Christie, a Scots merchant. The land on which it sits was once the garden of *94 Church*. The middle window on the first floor was originally a door, allowing the room within to be used for business while the family dwelt upstairs. Since 1908 it has been the rectory of St. Philip's Church.

The dwelling at *90 Church* is thought to have been built by Thomas Legare sometime after 1752. Three and one-half stories tall, the brick building is in the Georgian style and features a Regency piazza added in 1816 by George Macaulay. The middle window in the first level was a door. The main floor was probably used as a shop or counting house.

89-91 Church is a three story double tenement building of stuccoed brick dubbed "Cabbage Row" because early 1900's inhabitants set up vegetable stands on the sidewalks. The buildings are the legendary site of DuBose Heyward's "Catfish Row" of "Porgy," patterned after a heart-rending crippled black beggar, "Goat Cart Sammy" Smalls. Smalls and his goat cart begged coins on Charleston's Streets until shortly after World War I. Police records indicate the colorful character shot or shot at many women in his day. In the end, Sammy returned to his wife, Normie, not Bess, on "Jim" Island where he is buried "Crossways of the world" (North-South rather than the customary East-West, because he died as he lived, unrepentant).

92 Church Street

90 Church Street

89 · 91 Church Street

Church St.

Ninety-four Church, a three story hipped roof house, was built between 1760 and 1765 by John Cooper, a leader in the Colonial government and a patriot of the Revolution. From 1771 to 1799, Thomas Bee, an attorney, planter, delegate to the Continental Congress and U.S. Judge, owned the home. It has been mistakenly reported that Mr. Bee built the house in 1730. Gov. Joseph Alston, who was married to Theodosia Burr, daughter of Aaron Burr, Vice President of the United States under Thomas Jefferson, came into ownership a few years later. In 1832, the house was the site chosen by organizers of the Nullification Movement. The movement was designed to establish South Carolina as a sovereign, self governing state, and to nullify the unpopular Tariff Act of 1828. The Act led to the bloody Civil War during which the the Alexander Christie family owned the home.

93 and 95 Church are part of Church Street's later, and quieter history. Built in 1910 on the site of the Charleston Hydraulic Cotton Press Company, these two homes are examples of a row of two and one-half story frame Victorian residences.

94 Church Street

93 Church Street

95 Church Street

51 Meeting Street

39 Meeting Street

47 Meeting Street

Meeting St.

THE three story frame house of Andrew Hasell at *64 Meeting* was one of the last built on the street in the late 1700's. It features one of Charleston's classically elegant entry doors which leads to a two story piazza overlooking a walled garden.

Timothy Ford, an attorney from New Jersey, built the three and one-half story brick house with raised basement at *54 Meeting* in 1800. It still contains some of the finest Adamesque interior details in all of Charleston as well as a lovely garden.

60 Meeting was built as a double tenement apartment building in 1771. The eastern half is 64 Tradd Street. The building was remodeled in high Victorian style by Bertram Kramer, a bridge and wharf builder and general contractor, in 1893.

59 Meeting is a fine Georgian double house. Built in 1751 by a wealthy planter, William Branford, it is noted for fine cedar paneling and elaborate mantels. The double piazzas held up by graceful columns were built in 1830 by Brandford's grandson, Elias Horry, President of the South Carolina Railroad and the College of Charleston. The lower portico is finely detailed and the upper level is protected by fine ironwork.

64 Meeting Street

54 Meeting Street

54 Meeting Street

60 Meeting Street

59 Meeting Street

Meeting St.

Sixty-eight Meeting has served many purposes. The house was built in 1810 by John Cordes Prioleau, a factor and planter. It was his house slave who warned his master of a plot by a free black man to instigate a slave uprising in the city. Because of this information thirty-four people were hanged and the revolt was aborted. Later, from 1855-1862 the home was used as a school by Madame Rosalie Acelie Tongo. In 1886, Dr. Charles U. Shepard took up residence, using a small garden building as a laboratory for analytical chemistry. Dr. Shepard was also famous for his farm at Summerville where he grew tea commercially and for experimentation.

The three and one-half story home at *69 Meeting* was also the residence of a physician. Dr. John Ernest Poyas, Jr. constructed this home between 1796 and 1800. The home has lovely Adamesque interiors.

Manigault is one of the oldest names in Charleston history. Brothers Pierre and Gabriel arrived around 1695, fleeing religious persecution in France. Pierre's son, Gabriel, established the family name in Charleston through mercantile interests and his son, Gabriel, a talented amateur architect, continued the tradition. Young Gabriel designed *350 Meeting* for his brother Joseph in 1803. The house follows the elegance and simplicity associated with the designs of Robert Adam, a noted Scottish architect, creator of the Adamesque style. Owned by The Charleston Museum, the house is open to the public.

350 Meeting Street

69 Meeting Street

68 Meeting Street

Broad St.

ɪɴ Charleston's Grand Modell, Broad Street was just that, the broadest street. 92 Broad is referred to as Dr. David Ramsay's House. A physician and historian, Ramsay was deeply involved in the politics of the day, served as a war surgeon, and later wrote several volumes on Charleston, South Carolina and American history. He was murdered by a deranged patient in 1815.

Peter Bocquet, Jr., a merchant and planter, built the three and one-half story stuccoed brick home at 95 Broad on land gifted to him by his father in 1770. Bocquet owned several plantations and was active in the Revolution. The exterior of the house has been altered but the door on the left side dates from the Regency period, c. 1815-25. The wrought iron balcony is also considered to be original.

The home at 114 Broad was built by planter Ralph Izard in 1790 but remained unfinshed until 1829 when it was purchased by Col. Thomas Pickney Jr . Gen. Pierre G.T. Beauregard, used the house for headquarters for five months in 1863 during which time Confederate President Jefferson Davis was an honored guest.

95 Broad Street

92 Broad Street

114 Broad Street

Broad St.

ALTHOUGH built in 1760 by James Laurens, the house at *117 Broad* is referred to as the Edward Rutledge House. Rutledge, a signer of the Declaration of Independence, purchased the house from the Laurens estate in 1788. An attorney, Rutledge served as Governor of South Carolina in 1798. The house was Victorianized after 1885 by Capt. Frederick Wagener, a horse breeder and racer, and the exterior remodeled in the Colonial Revival style by Dr. Josiah Smith, after 1935.

The John Rutledge House Inn at *116 Broad Street* was built in 1763 for his bride, Elizabeth Grimke. Rutledge was a member of the South Carolina Assembly, the Stamp Act Congress and the Continental Congress. John Rutledge was co-author and signer of the U.S. Constitution. He was governor of the state from 1779-83, and an Associate and Chief Justice of the Supreme Court. In 1853, Thomas Norman Gadsten, a real estate broker and slave trader, bought and remodeled the house. He added the terra cotta window cornices and the wrought iron balconies. The ironwork is attributed to Christopher Werner and incorporates two of his favorite motifs: the palmetto tree of South Carolina and the United States eagle. The work is a combination of wrought and cast iron.

The house at *181 Broad* presents its charming facade from behind a classic stuccoed brick and wrought iron fence. Part of the lower piazza has been enclosed and converted into living space.

117 Broad Street

181 Broad Street

116 Broad Street

116 Broad Street

Charleston

EARLY every one of Charleston's streets and thoroughfares is rich in history. So many of Charleston's buildings have withstood wars, depression, hostile occupation and nature's worst in the form of fires, floods, earthquakes and hurricanes. Limehouse Street was named for the Limehouse family, through whose land the street was cut.

7 Limehouse, a small two and one half story brick home, is believed to have been built in 1830 by Robert Limehouse.

9 Limehouse was built by William Pinckney Shingler, a planter and cotton broker, in 1856. Financial problems forced him to sell the house almost immediately. By 1858, however, he had regained his fortune and built number 10 in a similar style.

Chalmers Street, once known as Chalmers Alley, was named for Dr. Lionel Chalmers, an eminent Scottish physician and scientist who did important work on tetanus and fevers.

John Breton built the Pink House, as it became known, at *17 Chalmers* in 1712. The tiny structure is believed to have been a tavern in Colonial days. It is constructed of Bermuda stone, a coral limestone imported in blocks from Bermuda. The building's gambrel roof is one of only a few surviving in Charleston.

7 Limehouse St.

17 Chalmers St.

9 Limehouse St.

Charleston

ORANGE Street was created along the eastern boundary of the Orange Garden, a park devoted to concerts under the fragrant shade of an orange grove. Alexander Petrie divided the property on the west side of the street into building lots for the nation's first racially integrated "subdivision." One of the lots was sold at public auction to "Amy, a free woman of color."

7 Orange was built on part of the site of the original orange grove by Col. Charles Pickney in 1769. Known as The Rivers House, this home had a number of owners before being acquired by M. Rutledge Rivers, a lawyer, educator and civic leader.

9 Orange is part of a three and one-half story double frame tenement built in 1770. This building was constructed when the term tenement meant a building with multiple dwellings and, with its gracious beauty, belays the more derogatory current meaning of the word.

9 Orange Street

3 Orange Street

7 Orange Street

7 Orange Street

Charleston

ARRE Street (pronounced Barry) was surveyed in 1770 and is named in honor of Isaac Barre, a sponsor of the cause against "taxation without representation." The Gov. Thomas Bennett House at *69 Barre* was built by Thomas Bennett, Jr., member of the S.C. House of Representatives, Speaker of the House, member of the Senate and Governor of South Carolina 1820-22. Built in 1825, the home originally looked out on Bennett's rice plantation, saw mills and mill ponds.

Adger's Wharf, one of several streets made by filling low lands, began its history as a "low water lot," exposed only at low tide. The land was filled to expand the ever growing city. In the 1830's and 40's, James Adger used the wharfs as the southern terminus of the first steamship line between Charleston and New York. This lucrative venture allegedly made him the richest man in South Carolina. In later years, large brick buildings lined the streets and were used as cotton warehouses and brokers' offices. At the end of port activity, the wharfs were abandoned and the buildings converted to residences and offices.

Lowndes Grove at *266 St. Margaret Street* was originally a plantation house built in 1786 by George Abbot Hall to replace one on another part of the property burned by British troops during the Revolution. Located on the Ashley River and beautifully landscaped by live oaks, "The Grove" was once the site of a duel between two generals, both of whom wished to be in charge of South Carolina troops.

69 Barre Street

69 Barre Street

35 N. Adger's Wharf

266 St. Margaret Street

Charleston

*L*ENWOOD Boulevard was named in honor of Gen. Leonard Wood, a U.S. Army commander in Charleston during World War I. Lenwood Boulevard was created as part of the Murray Boulevard development in the early 20th century and is graced with many lovely homes from that period.

Queen Street is one of the original streets in the Grand Modell. First called Dock Street for a boat dock at its swampy end, the street was renamed Queen for Caroline of Ansbach, the consort of George II. *22-28 Queen* is a notable row of three and one-half story stuccoed brick tenements built in the 1790's by the family of William Johnson, Associate Justice of the U.S. Supreme Court.

Bull Street was named for William Bull, a native South Carolinian who was the last to fill the Royally-appointed office of Lieutenant Governor.

The William Blacklock House, at *18 Bull*, was built in 1800 and is one of the nation's finest examples of Adamesque architecture. The house is constructed of Charleston grey brick, accented by stone trim. A double flight of iron railed stairs leads to the entry surrounded by sidelights and a fanlight with delicate traceries. The interior features excellent Adamesque woodwork and plasterwork and a graceful circular stair under an unusual vaulted ceiling. It is suggested that Gabriel Manigault, who served with Blacklock on the building committee for the bank, which is now City Hall, designed the house.

46 Lenwood Boulevard

30 · 28 · 26 · 24 · 22 Queen Street

18 Bull Street

Charleston

ALHOUN Street is named for John C. Calhoun, the "Great Nullifier." *Number 268*, a large frame house in the Greek Revival style, was built between 1838 and 1846 by Edward Sebring, president of the State Bank of South Carolina.

Ashley Avenue began as Lynch Street, named for Thomas Lynch. It was lengthened and changed names several times before becoming Ashley in 1897. The outstanding Greek Revival mansion at *178 Ashley* was built in 1850 by John Hume Lucas, a wealthy planter. It is a two-storied wood structure on a rusticated masonry basement. The columns on the front portico and the giant columns of the piazza have Tower of the Winds capitals, a form of Greek Cornithian.

The buildings at *2, 4 and 6 St. Michael's Alley* are classic examples of British style house placement. Each rests against the sidewalk and crowds against its neighbor, with blank wall sides.

Elizabeth Street was named for Elizabeth Wragg, daughter of Joseph Wragg and mother of architect Gabriel Manigault. The Aiken-Rhett House, at *48 Elizabeth Street*, was built by John Robinson in 1817 as a simple double house. Governor William Aiken acquired the property in 1832 and remodeled the house in Greek Revival Style to the expansive 23 rooms seen today. Confederate General Beauregard used the house as his headquarters during the bombardment of Charleston and President Jefferson Davis was the guest of honor at a dinner when he visited in November, 1863. Owned by The Charleston Museum, the house is open to the public.

268 Calhoun Street

6 · 4 · 2 St. Michael's Alley

178 Ashley Avenue

48 Elizabeth Street

95 East Bay

Rainbow Row

East Bay

AILOR and livery stable owner Benjamin Dupre built the two story wooden home on a high brick basement at *317 East Bay* between 1803 and 1805. The home features lovely Adamesque details throughout the interior.

The stately mansion at *631 East Bay* is called the Faber-Ward House. It was built around 1832 by Henry F. Faber. The architecture was copied from Andrea Palladio, a noted Italian designer of the 16th century. The stone arches which support the pillared piazza are each 15 feet tall. Joshua Ward, a wealthy and famous rice planter as well as South Carolina's Lieutenant Governor, purchased the home from Faber. No expense was spared in the construction of this home and materials such as Italian marble and mahogany imported from the tropics saw lavish usage. The house fell from grace when Union troops occupied the city, converting the mansion into a hotel for recently emancipated slaves. The hotel failed and the house again became a private residence for a while before being turned into apartments and sliding into a post World War II decline. Most of its neighboring mansions did not survive this era. Today only one remains, along with the sad shell of another. *631 East Bay* has been turned into an office building with three apartments. The house however, still stands as mute testimony to the era when Charleston was the Queen city of the South.

71 East Bay

73 East Bay

317 East Bay

631 East Bay